Amy's Maine Coloring Book

Amy Pollien

To all the people who saw a woman in the road staring intently at their home over the edge of her sketchbook, and simply shrugged and went about their day without thinking too much about it.

Where Are We?

Maine is a wonderful place to be an artist. The weather is unpredictable and can be challenging in the winter, but those storms and frigid temperatures have shaped the rocks into intriguing shapes and scoured their edges clean for painters to admire and photographers to record. That landscape is harsh but incredibly beautiful.

Humans have lived along these shores for a long time. Some of the houses in this book were built by ship captains and fishermen during the 19th century but the small coves and creek beds along the coast show evidence of human habitation for at least a thousand years. Their shell middens, hearths, and grave sites dot the map of the coastline in the same places where the first white arrivals found shelter and abundant food, and settled into the harbors and factory towns pictured in this book.

So, welcome to the Maine landscape! Here the spruce trees are dark green, the cold Atlantic Ocean waters look gray, and the granite rocks are pink, stained with iron deposits in the soil. I have included a color reproduction of the finished work from these drawings for reference, but follow your own muse to make them your own.

The title of each drawing includes map coordinates, so follow your GPS to create your own images of beautiful Downeast Maine and Acadia National Park.

A Note about Technique

Colored pencil is the most popular medium used in coloring books today. Several brands will provide a richer tone if you blend them with water and a damp brush or dampen the paper first..

Wax crayons or oil pastels make a strong statement and can be used almost as a gesture in the small spaces of these images. Think about the technique of Pointillism pioneered by Seurat and others in the 1840's and make short individual marks that blend visually into a composition. Or blend oil pastels with a solvent such as turpentine for a smooth, vibrant effect.

Using oil or acrylic paint is also a possibility. Remove a page from this book and use clear shellac to seal the surface. (Gluing the page to a stiff backing with water-based glue or more shellac may be helpful.) When the shellac is thoroughly dry, it will be safe to paint over with any solvent-based pigment.

For needlepoint or embroidery, remove a page and fasten it to your base fabric. Use a poncing wheel and dry pigment to transfer the major features of the image to the fabric and then spray with fixative.

Whatever the medium, please enjoy these images and your role in making a final product that is unique and wholly your own.

Seawall, Late Afternoon, Low Tide

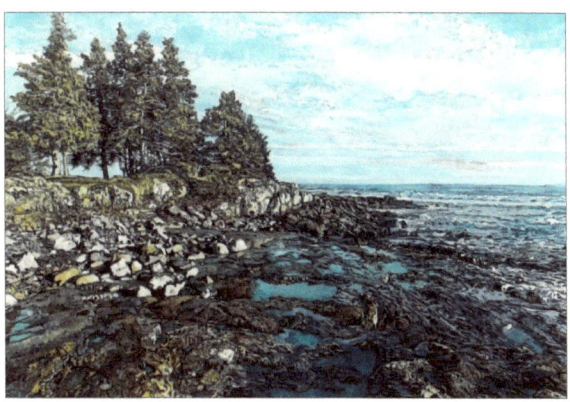

Southwest Harbor, 44.238407, -68.303759

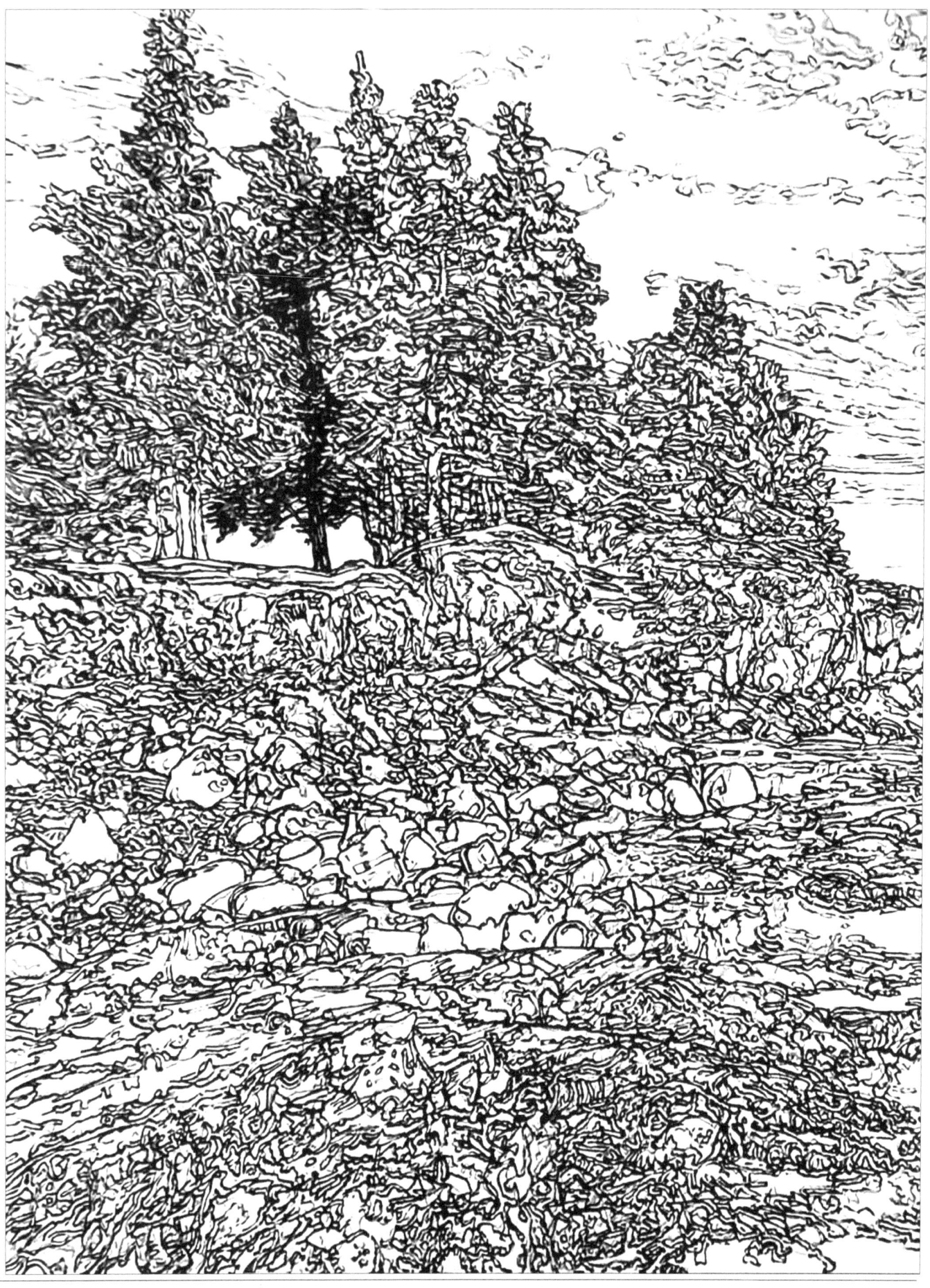

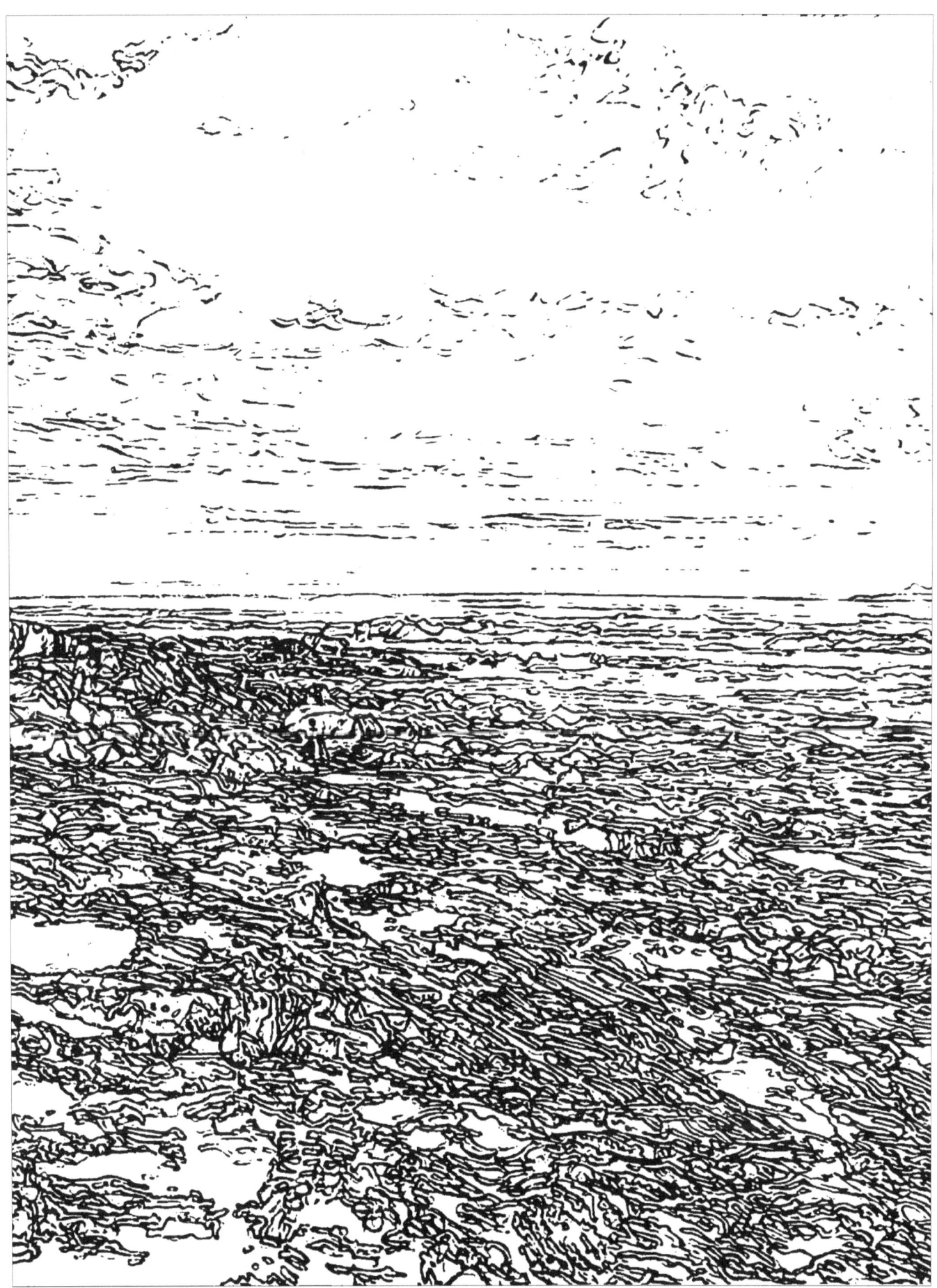

Bass Harbor Cliffs

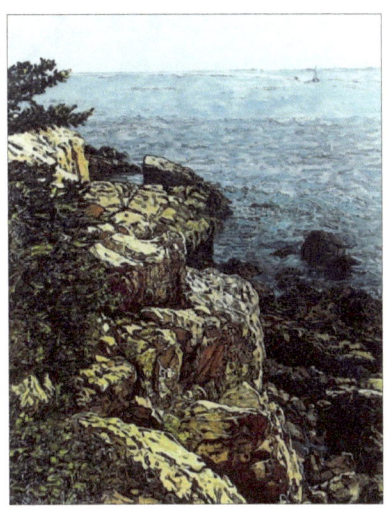

Bass Harbor Light, Acadia National Park, 44.222687, -68.336579

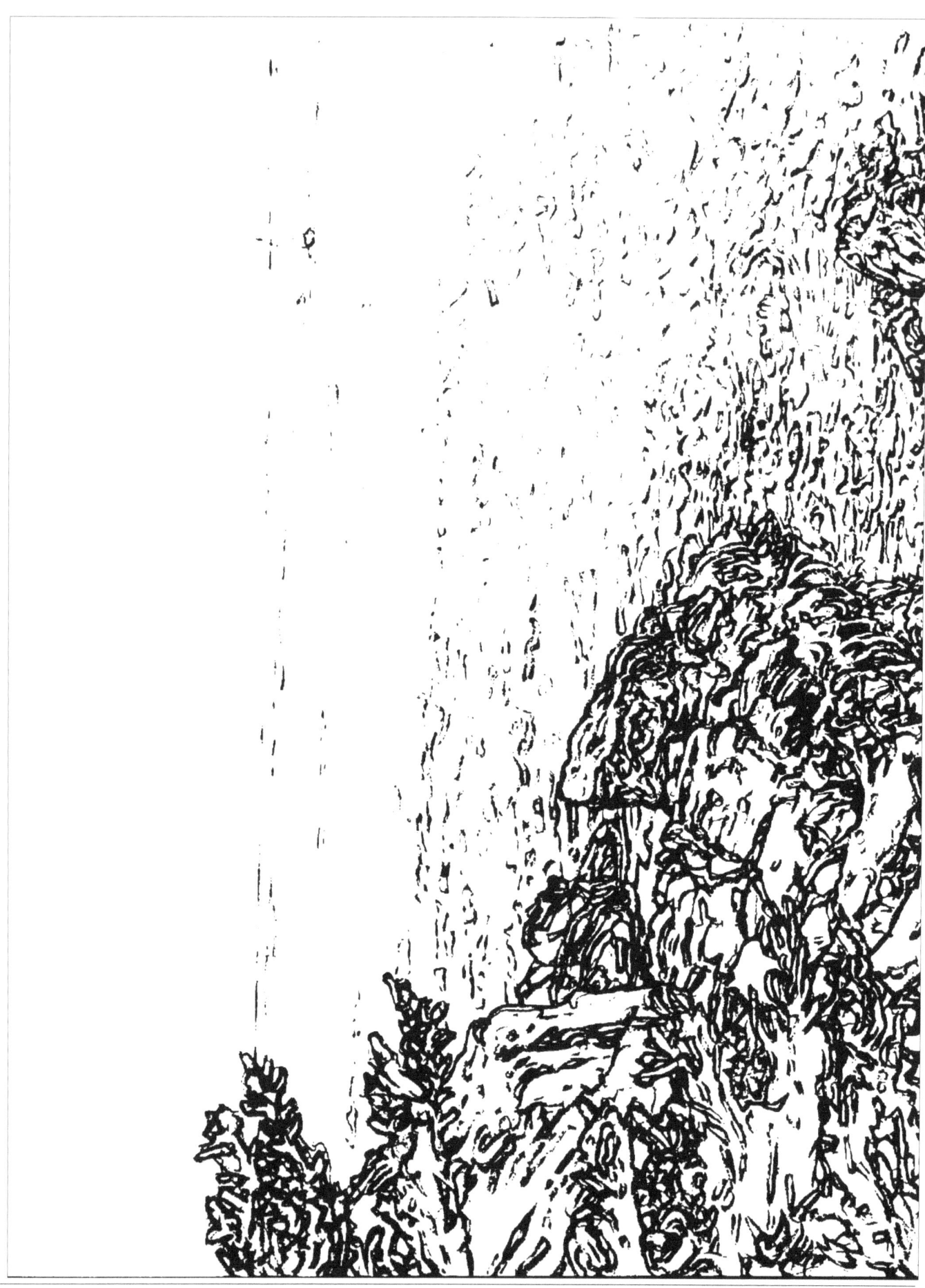

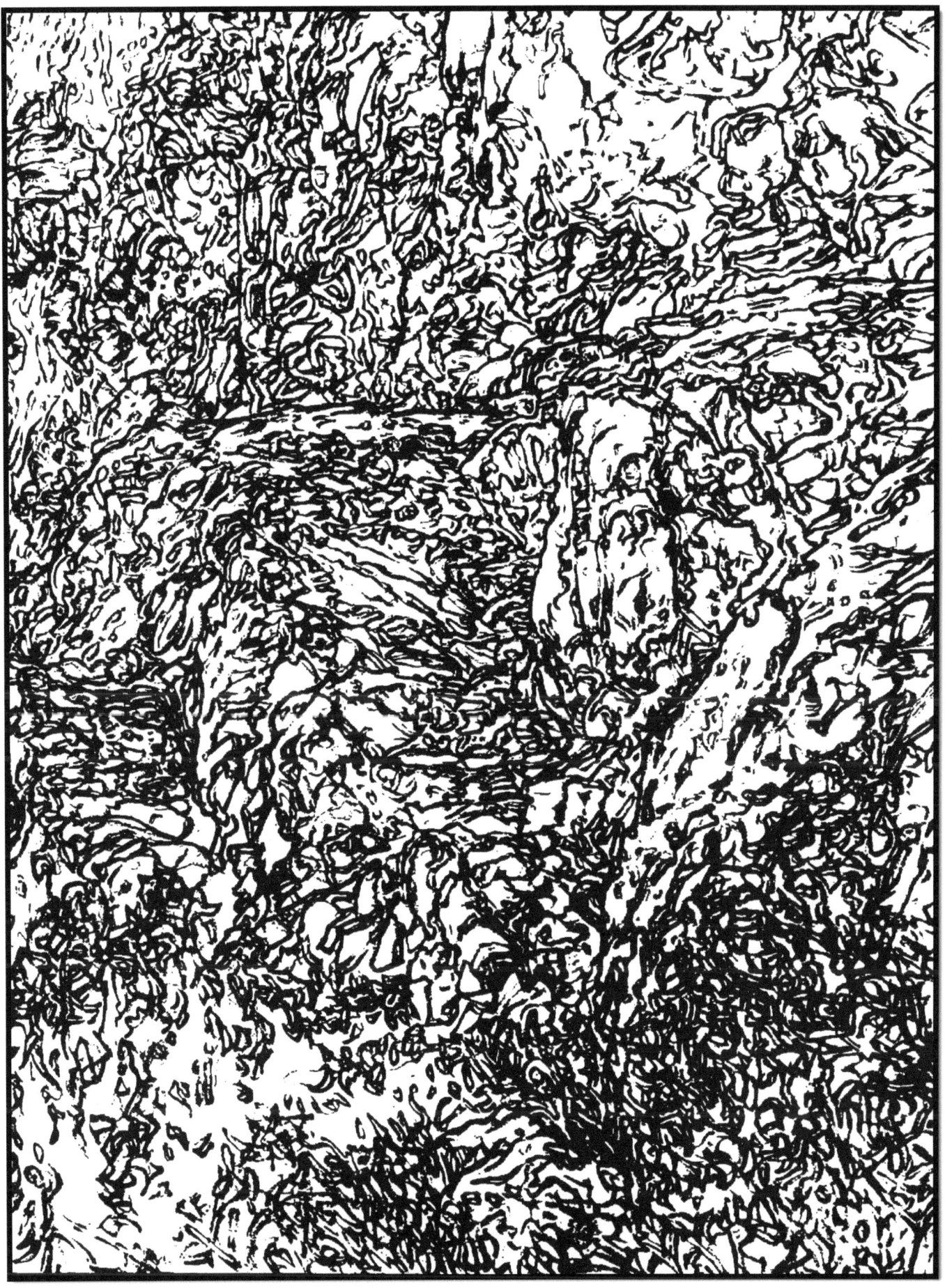

Hill House, Stonington

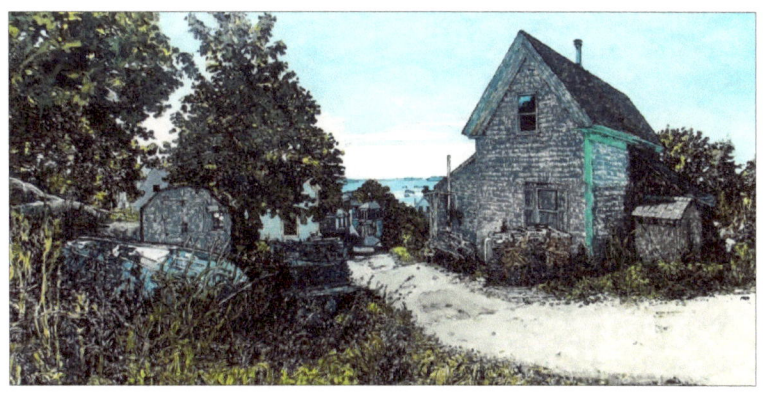

Stonington Harbor, 44.152864, -68.652433

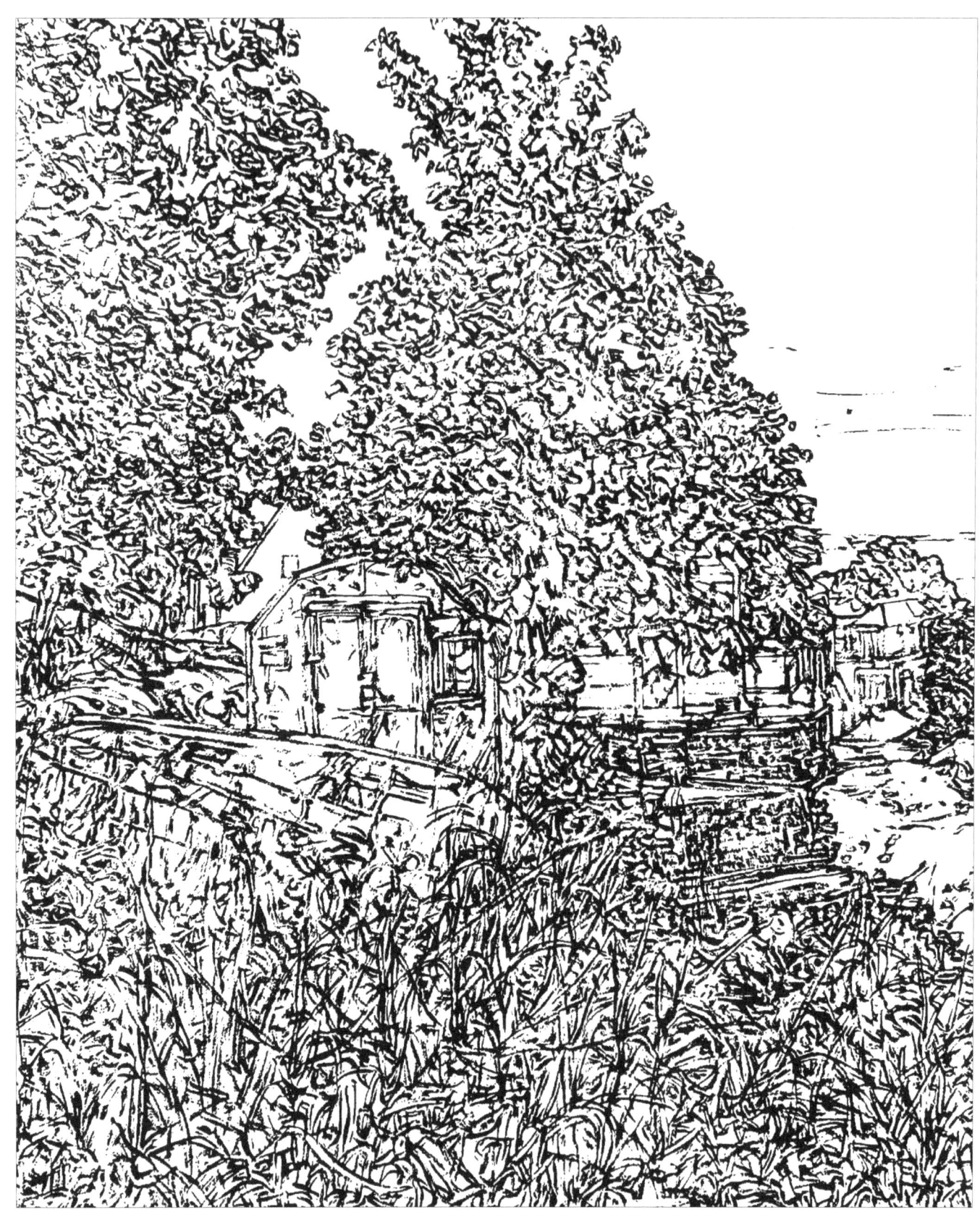

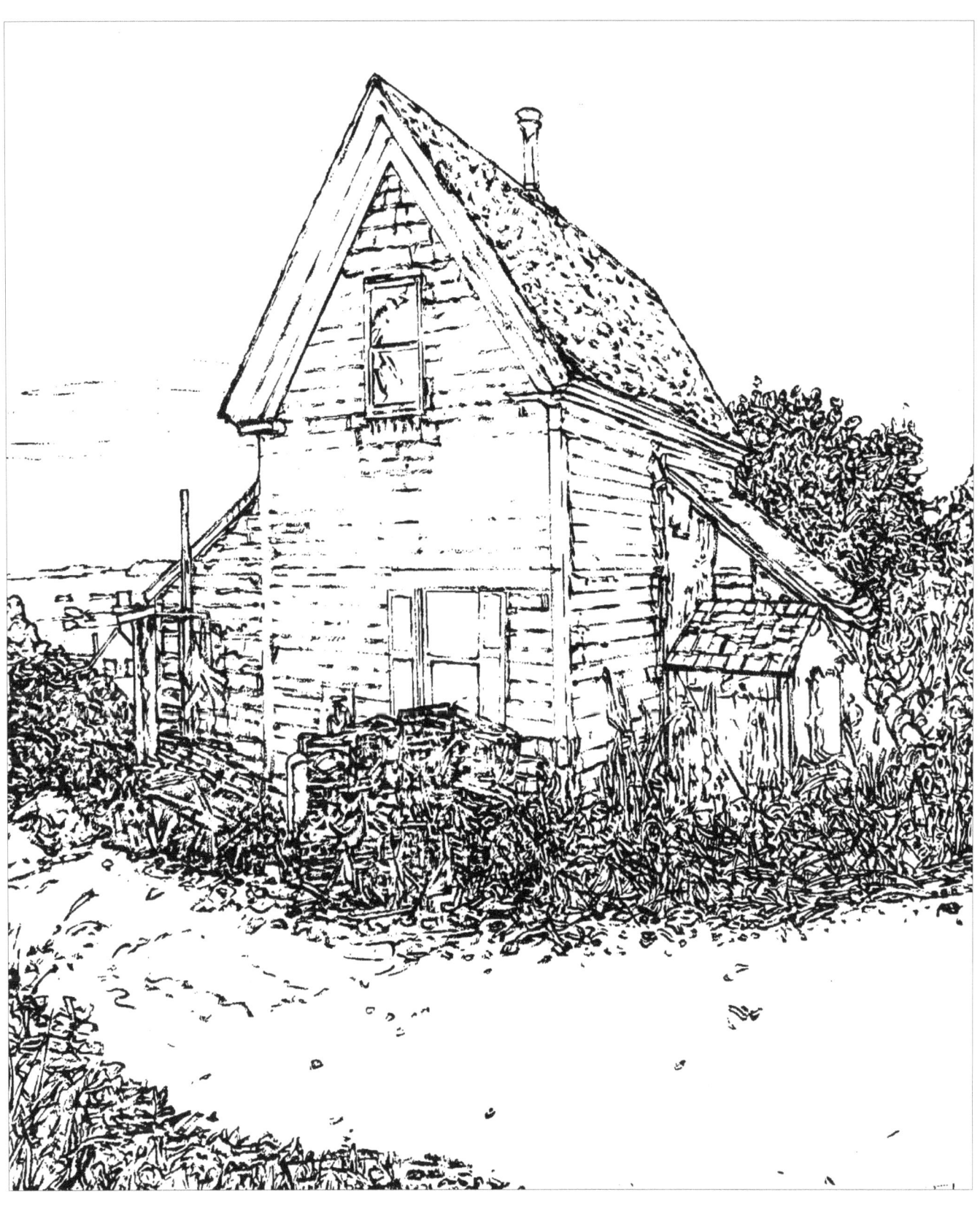

Bald Porcupine Island, Frenchman Bay

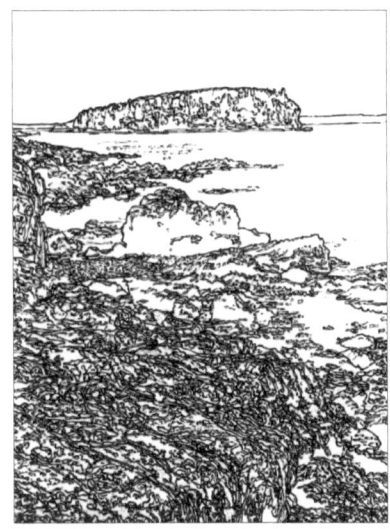

Bar Harbor, 44.386442, -68.181662

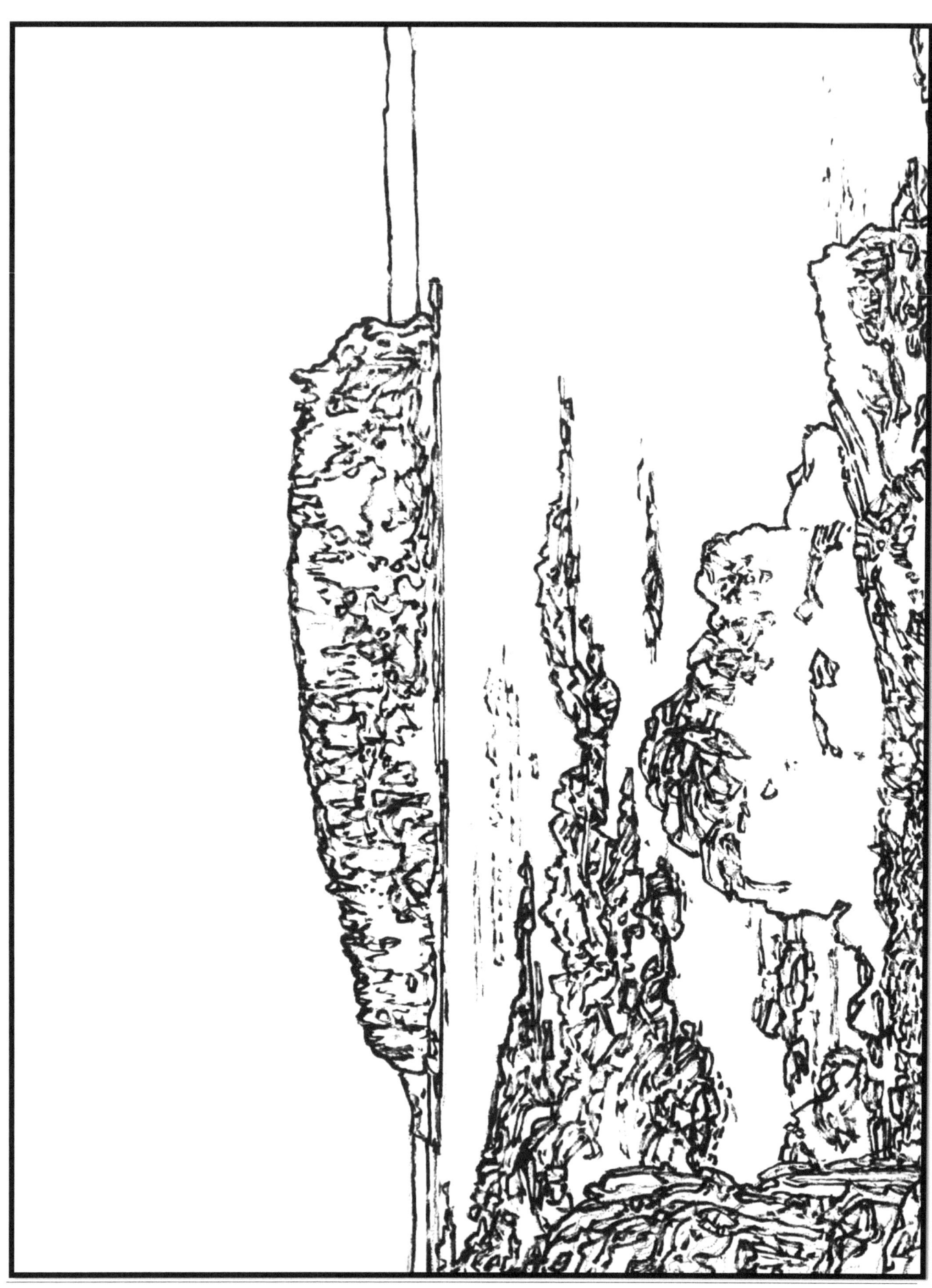

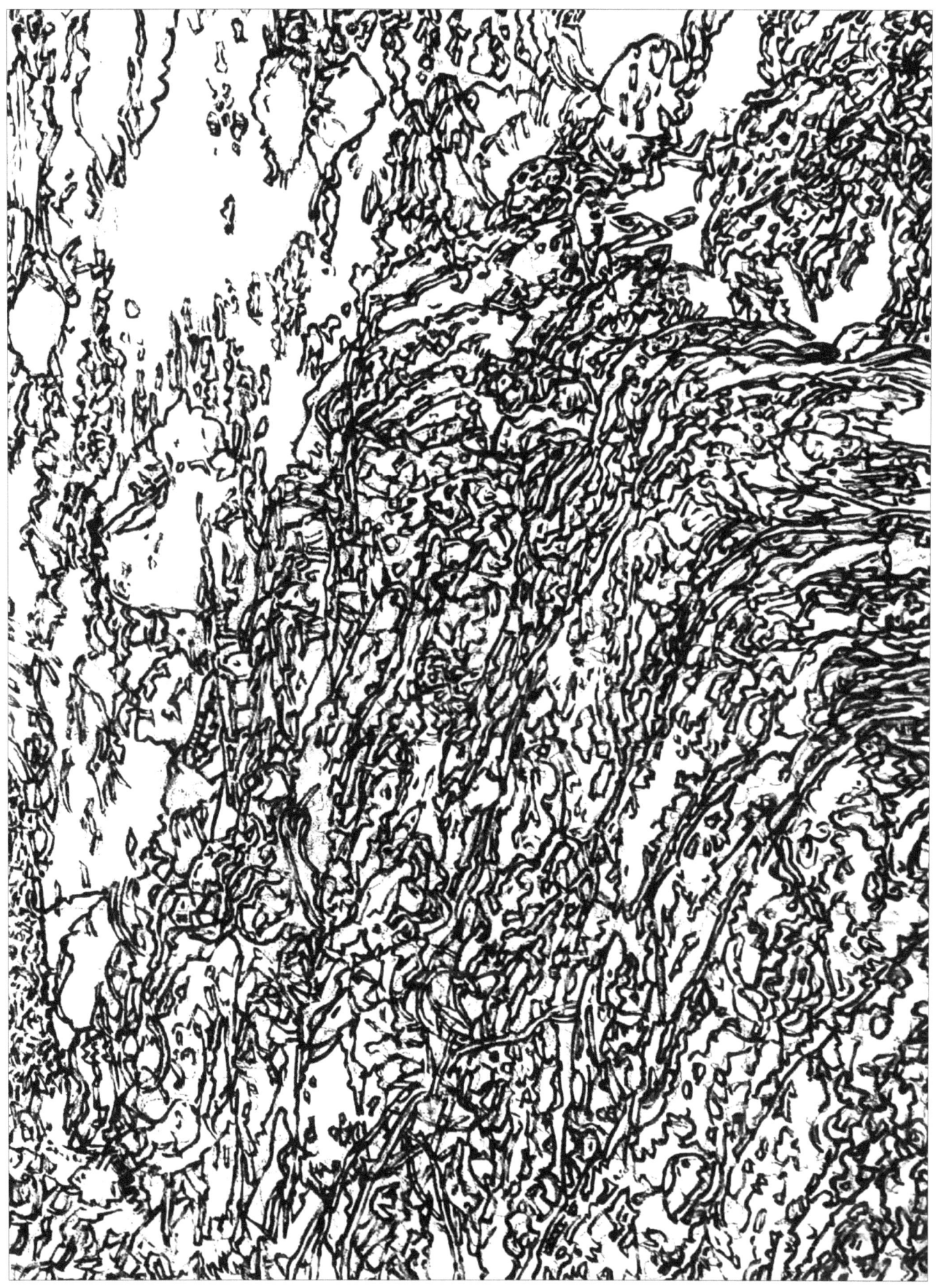

The Pickets

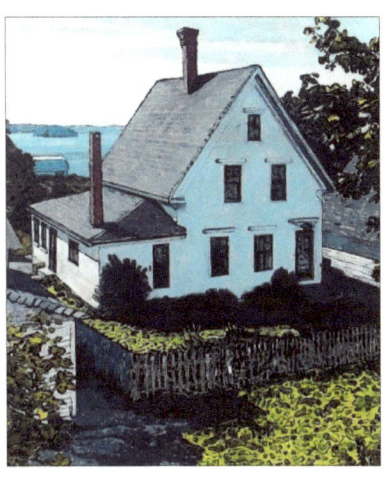

Stonington, 44.152864, -68.652433

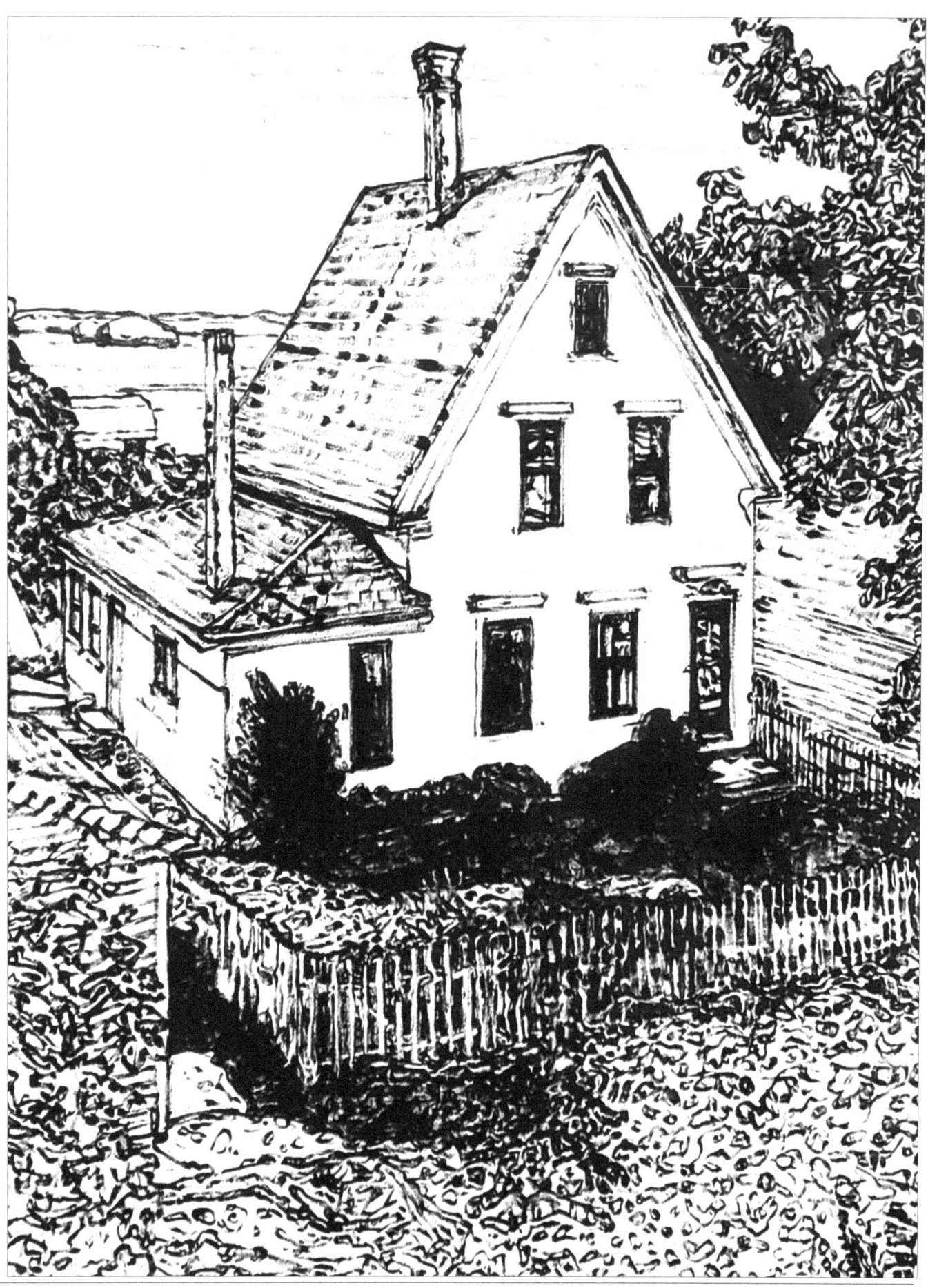

Myrtle Avenue, Bar Harbor, Dusk

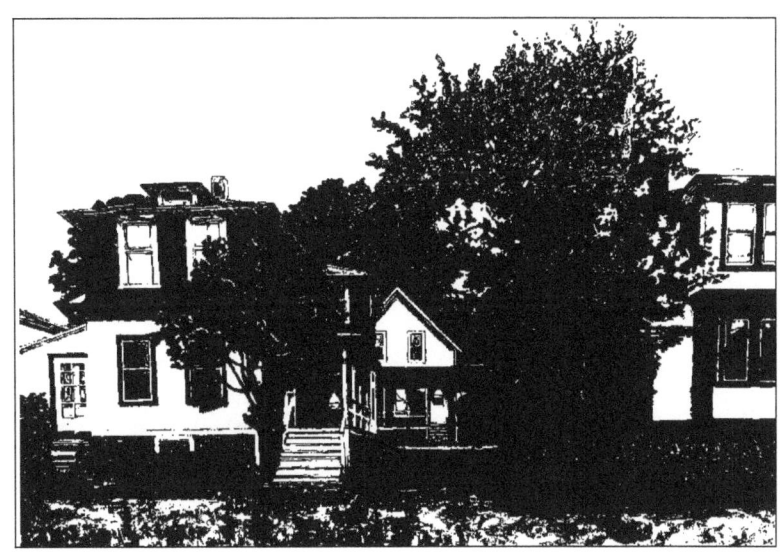

Bar Harbor, 44.387642, -68.213827

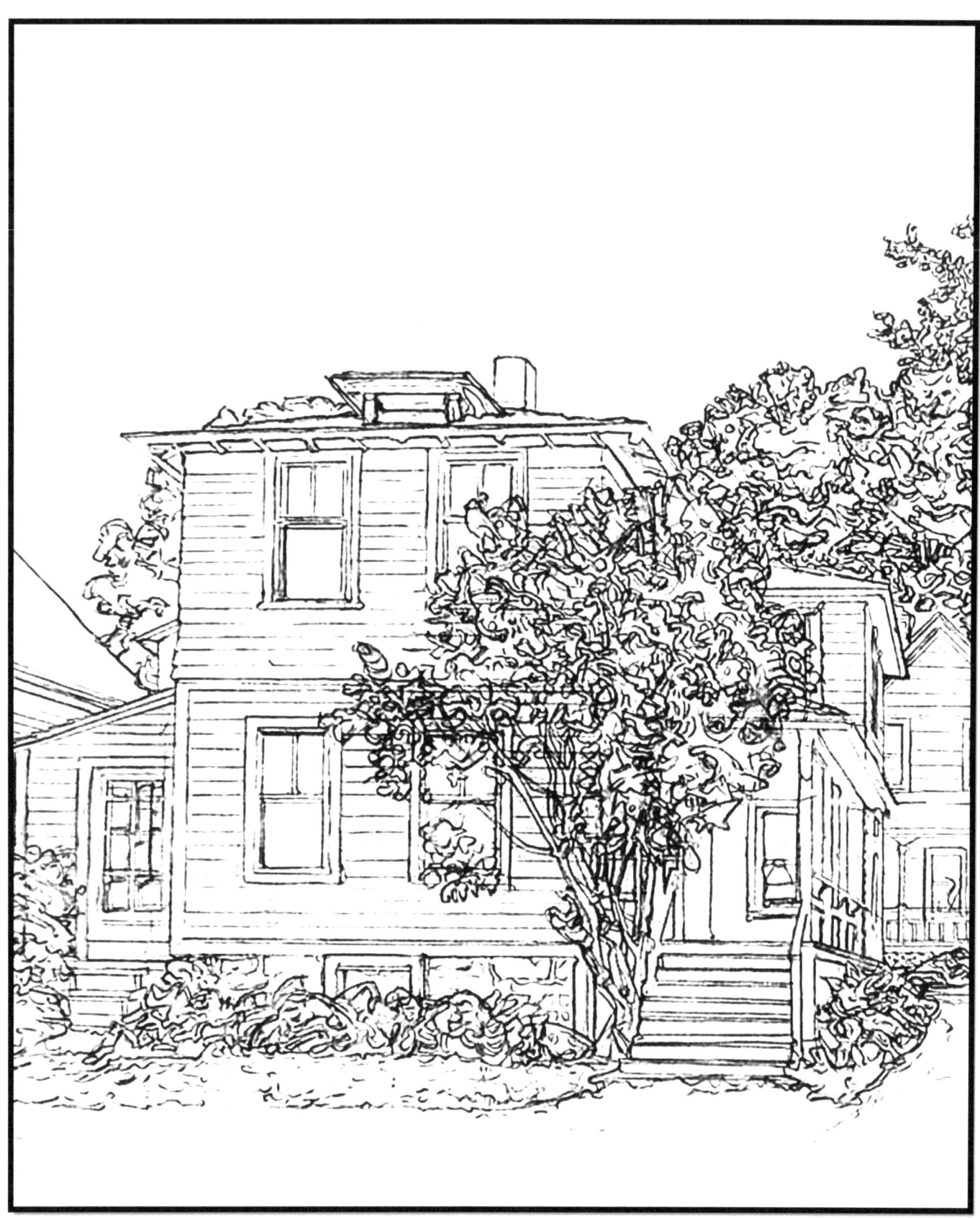

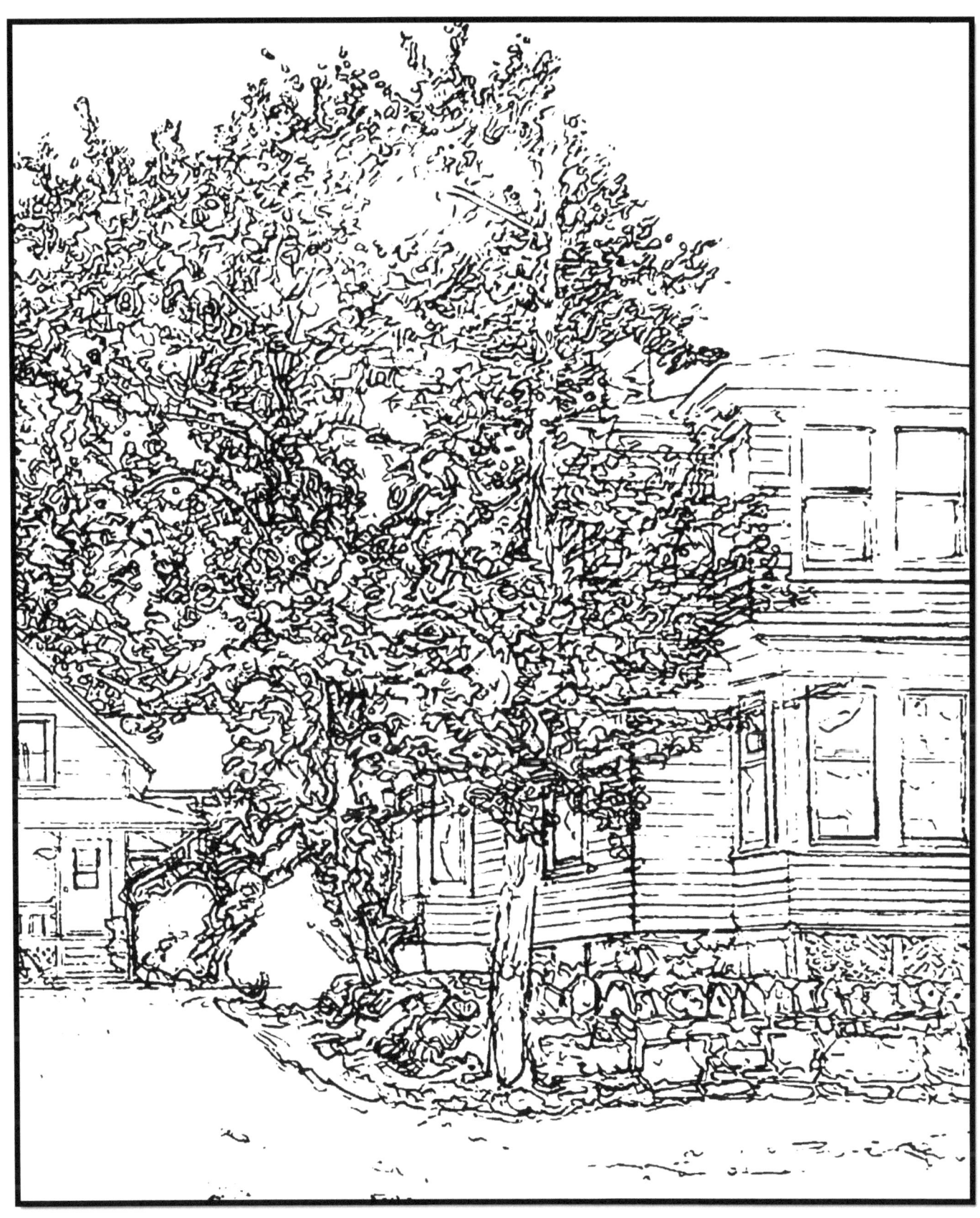

Bass Harbor Trees

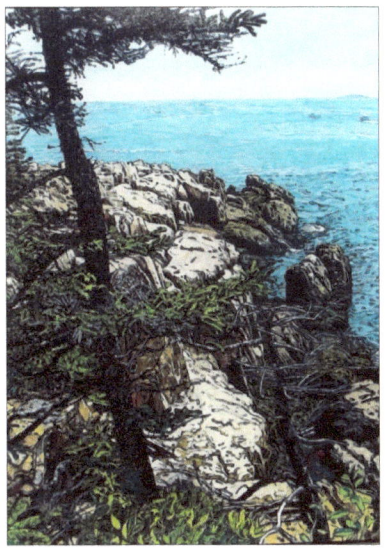

Bass Harbor Light, Acadia National Park, 44.222687, -68.336579

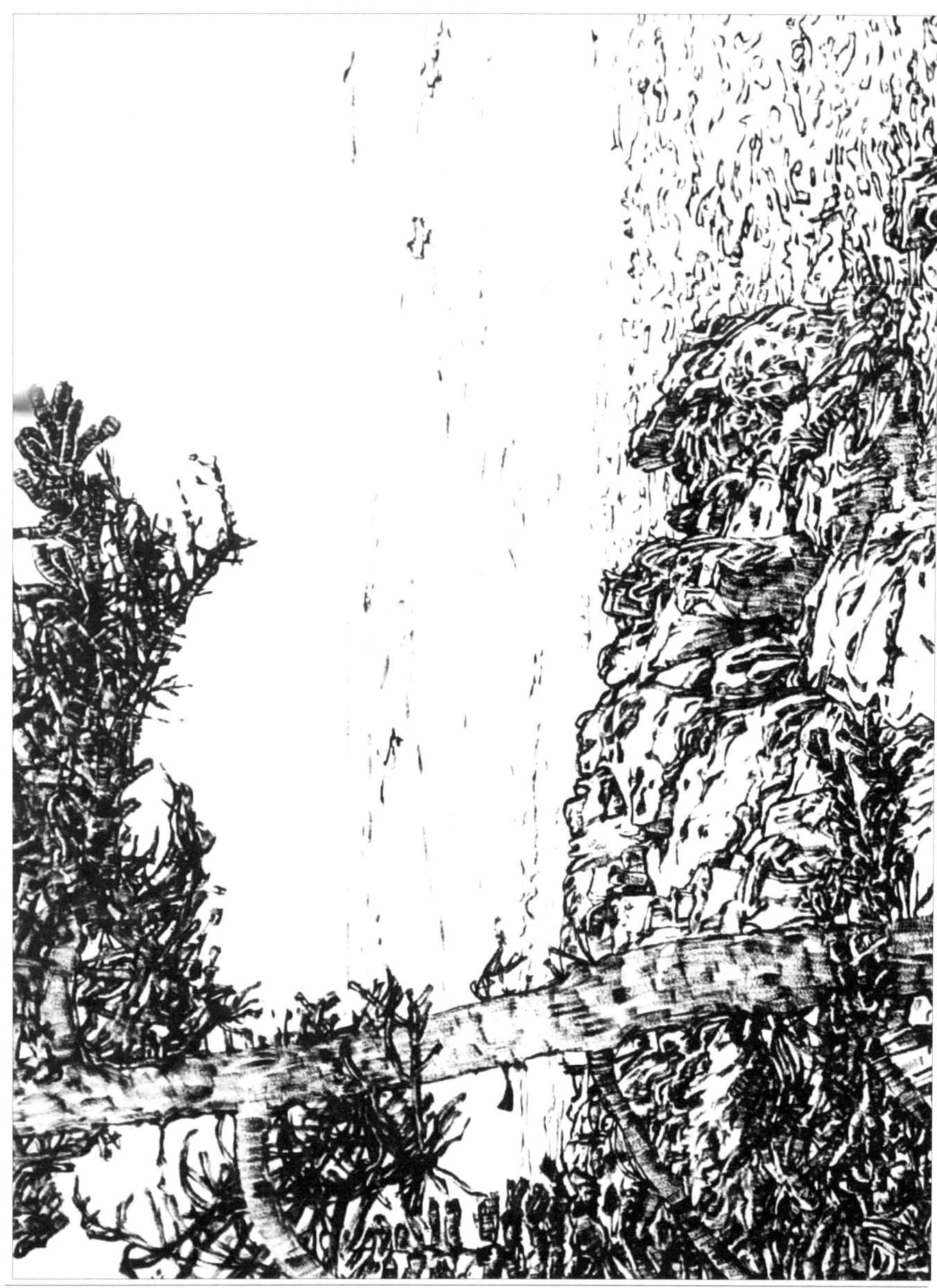

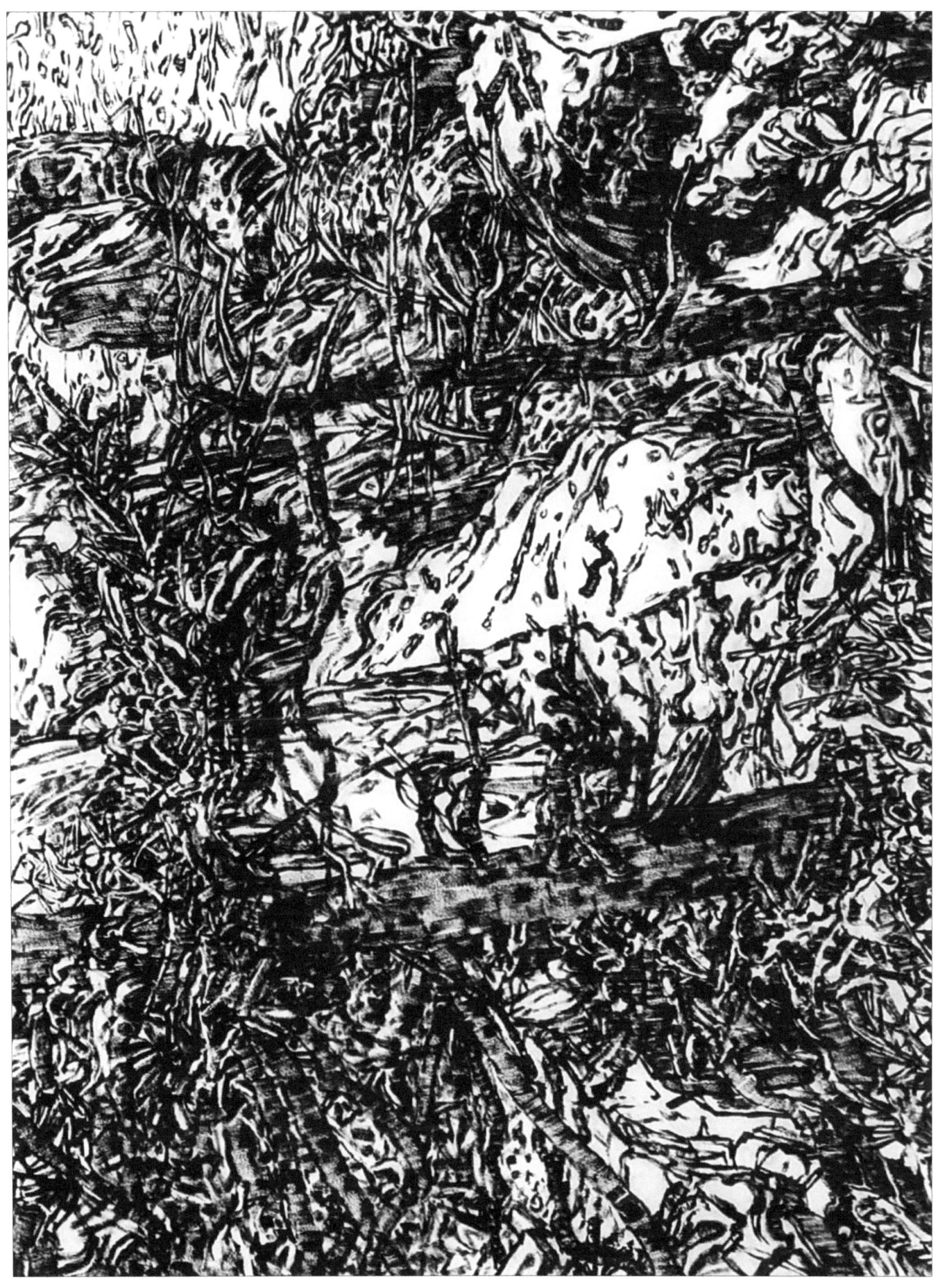

Stonington Harbor View

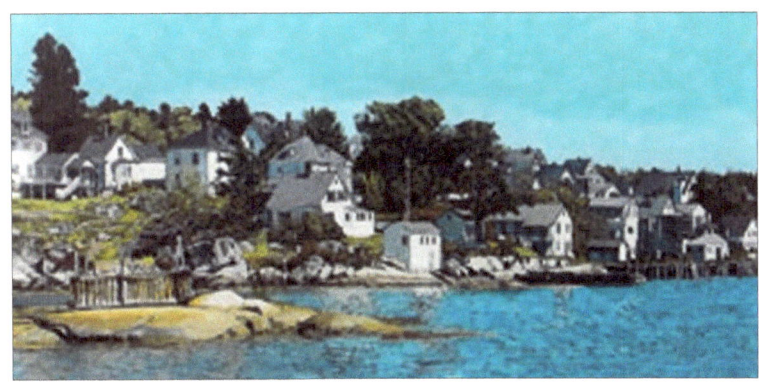

Stonington Harbor, 44.152864, -68.652433

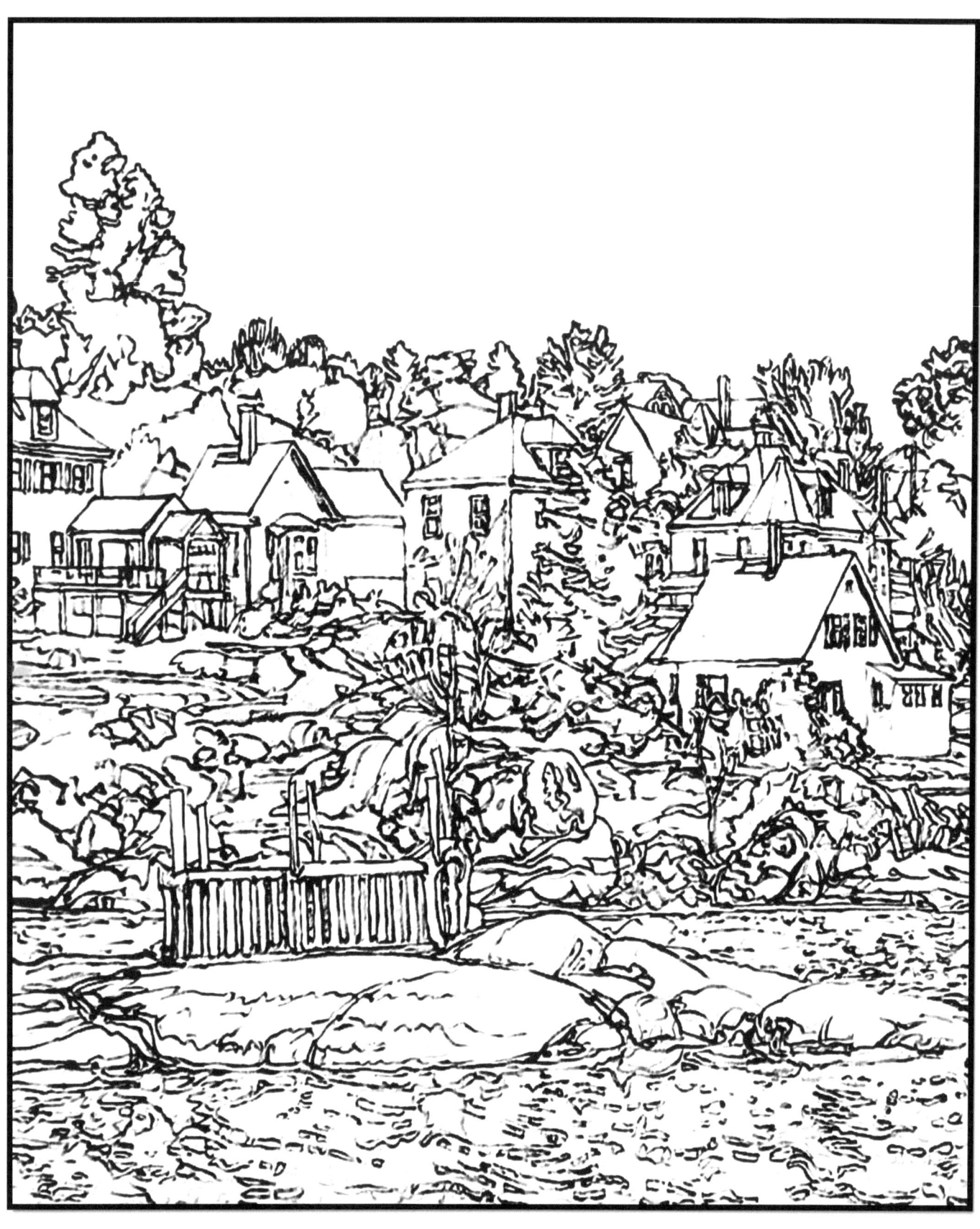

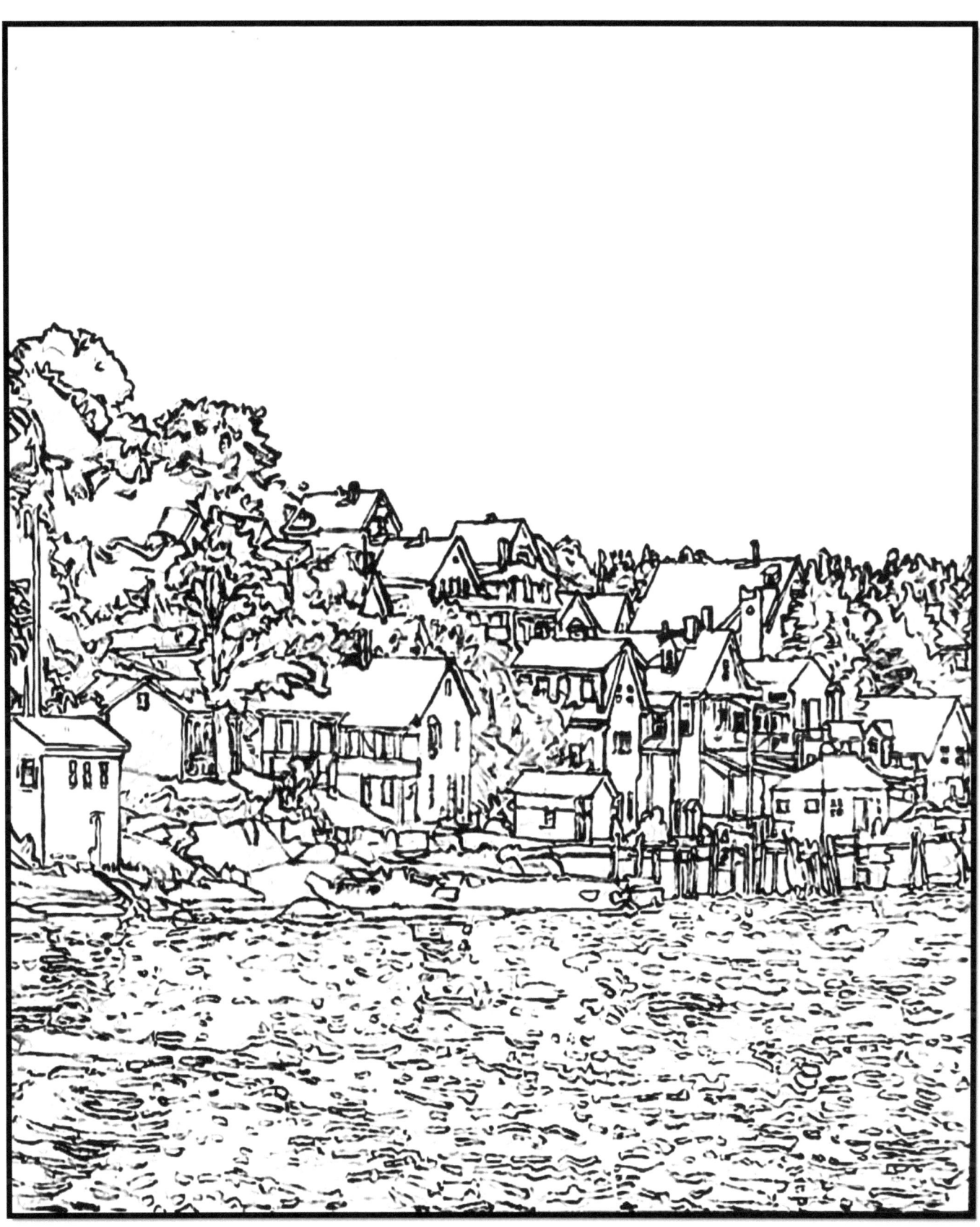

www.ingramcontent.com/pod-product-compliance
Lightning Source LLC
Chambersburg PA
CBHW040754200526
45159CB00025B/2090